MW00795668

To Jessica
Best Wishes!

Free Ride *to College*

A Guide to Grooming Your Kids For a Full Academic Scholarship

Volume 1-First Edition
"Rising Senior/Senior Year"

November 2013
Published by Free Ride to College Media
P.O. Box 361882
Columbus, Ohio 43236

Email: Info@FreeRide2College.com

Free Ride to College: A Guide to Grooming Your Kids
For a Full Academic Scholarship

ISBN: 978-0-9911979-0-3

First Publication November 2013 in the United States of America

Table of Contents

Acknowledgements

I have a confession to make; I really did not raise and educate my children. A village raised my children. The village was their father, grandparents, aunts, uncles, cousins, godparents and close friends. Raising children is not an easy task and there is really no manual that addresses every issue that will come up. The best way to raise children is to employ the wisdom of the village you have at hand, and that is what I did. I want to take this opportunity to thank the village that helped raise and educate my children.

First, I want to thank my husband for his unwavering support. He is the absolute best husband and an even better father. He was the captain of our team as we raised our children. His firm but gentle demeanor made it possible for me to keep our children focused by reinforcing our rules for education and work ethics.

I am so grateful to my children's grandparents who showered them with wisdom and unconditional love. Along with that came lots of valuable life lessons, which only a grandparent's love can nurture.

I'd like to acknowledge their grandma in North Carolina who was pretty, kind and charismatic with an outgoing personality. She did not meet any strangers, so people loved being around her. My children learned a lot from their grandma about meeting people (folk up North call it networking). During their visits in the summers, she showed them how to live off the land; raise chickens and grow a bountiful garden. When they would return to Ohio they would inform me, "Mom, we did not have to go to the store to buy things to eat at Grandma's!"

She showed them how to harvest food. She would send the kids out to pick and shell peas and gather vegetables from the garden for dinner. They learned how to wring a chicken's neck, dip it in scalding water to de-feather it, clean it, cut it up and fry it in a pan. She also taught the girls how to cook, and of course, bake a cake from scratch, by hand without using a mixer.

I also want to express my gratitude to Aunt Mary who taught the girls about hair, jewelry and clothes. She owned the largest beauty salon in the state of Alabama and was the first black cosmetologist to be appointed to the Alabama State Board of Cosmetology, ironically by the late Governor George Wallace. She even taught me how to care for the girls' hair. She was fancy; she wore fancy clothes, adorned her house with fancy furniture and framed her pretty face with fancy hairdos. My aunt was the girls' role model on how to dress and how to act like ladies.

Then there is Grandpa who lives in Michigan. Grandpa is now eighty-seven years old, but still very active. As an Alumni of Talladega College in Alabama, he has always emphasized education. He has driven my children all over the states east of the Mississippi River to learn the geography and history of the United States. Almost every summer as they were growing up, Grandpa shared his resources and wisdom with his grandkids, traveling the country. One of the highlights of traveling with their grandpa was while visiting New York City. "Mom, we learned that Grandpa was the first black person from the state of Alabama appointed to West Point in the 1940's by Congressman Adam Clayton Powell," my kids exclaimed with proudness.

All of my siblings have spent priceless time with my children, adding to the educational enrichment of their nieces and nephews. For that I am appreciative.

Thanks to my many cousins and relatives who have added to my children's life in so many priceless and beautiful ways.

And last but not least, their Godparents have been such an amazing support in every aspect of their lives as well.

Thanks to everybody, the entire village, that helped me raise and educate my children. I really could not have done it without you!

From the Author

Free Ride to College: A Guide to Grooming Your Kids For a Full Academic Scholarship is a decade of hard work, research and experience of how I raised my children-one who was labeled as a candidate for special education, another labeled as having Attention Deficit Hyperactivity Disorder (ADHD) and the youngest who was almost legally blind-to earn full academic scholarships to college. Despite what my children were labeled as or tried to be labeled as, they all became writing and math whizzes and matriculated in engineering at college.

I have been called a tiger mom and a strict teacher, but in no way do I consider myself a tiger mom. I never went to the types of extremes tiger moms have been labeled to have gone to. Simply put; I'm N. J. Richards, a certified science teacher in the State of Ohio, but more important than what I do is who I am. I am a parent raising children in a society that makes attending college difficult due to the financial obstacles.

Since I graduated from college in the 1980's, the cost of a college education has risen an unbelievable 1,200%. If you are a parent or grandparent with a child entering kindergarten, it is estimated that college in the years 2025 through 2030 will cost, on the low end, $76,000 per year. Most would agree that in order to live a fairly comfortable life and excel in a chosen career field, having at least a bachelor's degree is still the quintessential credential to obtain. In fact, currently people that hold a bachelor's degree earn about one million dollars more in a lifetime than a high school graduate. Clearly, higher education is an absolute must. The business of obtaining a higher education is competitive; right down from gaining entrance to college to obtaining scholarships to fund higher education. Life is competitive and so is getting a full ride to college.

Accordingly, if we want our children to be able to keep up, we must start when they are young and mold them to be competitive students. My background as a teacher and parent of three children that were awarded full academic scholarships to college has given me years of experience and expertise in building competitive student profiles. It is that student profile in which higher education institutions will base the student's admission on as well as what scholarship committees will base their award distributions on.

These profiles made my children competitive students and ultimately they received offers of over one and a half million dollars in scholarship money combined. Consequently, I have saved close to a half a million dollars in college expenses. In addition, they all matriculated in engineering; my son Carlos, industrial, my daughter Vanessa, mechanical, and my daughter Nicole, chemical engineering. Now that I have an empty nest, I am on a mission to help other families achieve free rides to college too.

Free Ride to College: A Guide to Grooming Your Kids For a Full Academic Scholarship will lay out the importance of raising and building up a child with the goal of achieving a competitive student profile. It is a process that begins at birth to elementary, to middle and through high school. If you are a student looking for help navigating the college application and scholarship map, which can be very puzzling and filled with detours and obstacles, you are in the right place. I put *Free Ride to College: A Guide to Grooming Your Kids For a Full Academic Scholarship* together as a step by step guide of information and resources. Although I do include various scholarships in Free Ride to College, it is not simply a list of scholarships, but rather a guide that will show you how to build a competitive student profile in order to help achieve some of those scholarships.

There are many resources that provide lists of scholarships, but lists alone will not get you scholarships. There are also other books and resources out there where the author will tell you what they did and/or what you need to do. What makes Free Ride to College different and unique is that I don't just tell you what I did and what you need to do; I show you! I equip you with the tools, techniques, information and resources that can allow you to have a well-planned and thought out process to aid you in acquiring scholarships.

Each edition will provide directions to access millions of dollars in scholarship opportunities. Every year many of these funds go untapped because the scholarship committees don't find enough worthy candidates and people get overwhelmed by the daunting task of securing the funds. It's so easy to get lost. But what if you allow someone who has already been down that road into the driver's seat to lead the way? Well, picture me as kind of like that chauffer behind the wheel taking you to your destination…or at least points you in the right direction.

In this first edition of *Free Ride to College*, I focus on the rising high school senior and senior year and show you how to market your student profile. I touch upon the matters urgent for seniors when beginning this journey. My hope, though, is that you will travel with me through this edition and future editions that will show you step by step how to build a competitive student profile and exploit the extra time you have in order to build your profile. The next issue will focus on the rising high school junior and junior year. It, as well as future editions, will go more into depth and details and promises to be filled with valuable knowledge, information, tips and advice about building a competitive student profile.

So buckle up, and let's begin the journey!

-N. J. Richards

On Your Ride, Do the Work, Be Patient and Keep the Faith

I will never forget the feelings of anguish, anxiety and distress I felt a week before my baby daughter, Nicole's, high school graduation. I had a possible twenty-two thousand dollar college tuition bill staring me in the face and one for forty-two thousand dollars underneath it. I put the lower one on top, hoping she would choose to attend the cheaper school, if you can call twenty-two thousand dollars cheap. Then I thought about the fact that she was majoring in engineering and would probably take five years to complete that program instead of the usual four. So I was really looking at a possible one hundred and ten thousand dollar college tuition. I was frantic. Where was I going to get that kind of money? Even if I had it, my house was in need of so many repairs: a worn out kitchen floor, a bathroom that needed remodeling and my car was on the threshold of breaking down for good. I thought, I can get a second job. But then I had a second thought: But I am not that young anymore. I'd have to have energy to work every day all day. I wasn't sure if I had the energy for that. I'd been out of the nine to five business for many years. This was a quandary I never wanted to find myself in, but at that point, I knew I had to do whatever it took.

I had saved a total of fifty dollars in Nicole's college savings. I know it is shameful, so shameful that my oldest daughter said that I shouldn't even confess to that. But that was my reality. Of course once upon a time her college fund had a few more zeros, but life happens! All of my other kids had gone to college on full academic rides and majored in engineering, so that was five years of college expenses for two kids at about twenty-two thousand dollars a year times five. That was over a quarter of a million dollars I got saved from having to pay in college expenses. I'd truly been spoiled to say the least.

It had been a long road getting my baby girl to the point of even being accepted into the colleges of her choice, and now it was about to become a bumpy one. I do not want to scare you off or overwhelm you in our travels. But I will give you a heads-up that in getting my children free rides to college, I did meet a snag or two. If you are a middle class family, as my family is, there is less aid available to you. The Free Application for Federal Student Aid (FAFSA) did not award us any grant money and we only qualified for about five thousand dollars in loan money, which would have to cover two students because I would now have two kids in college at the same time. One had already recently graduated (Thank God!). In addition, I looked at the time, energy, money and sacrifices I had spent on applying for scholarships over the last six months for my youngest child. I was exhausted.

The parent and fighter in me knew that if I'd done it once, then turned around and did it twice, that the third time would be a charm. Although my other child in college had a full ride, there are always miscellaneous expenses that add up. Even when we have full coverage insurance, somehow we always end up with some kind of out of pocket expense. The same can go for college as well. So by no means do I suggest that just because you are setting the GPS to guide you to a free ride to college should you not maintain some type of college savings funds (reserve tank;-).

Nicole had been awarded monies, but not enough to cover the twenty-two or forty-two thousand dollars needed to attend the state or prestigious private college, respectively, she had been accepted to. Up to that point I had never had to pay for college. Fear can either paralyze you or make you run just that much faster. I refused to be paralyzed, finding myself stalled on the side of the road.

I kept the faith that all of our hard work in securing tuition would pay off as well as continued to tap into all the resources available to me. We had done our due diligence.

We applied for at least sixty scholarships, wrote about one hundred essays, and produced several videos for scholarship competitions. Yes, I said videos. I thought outside the box and so should you. The following link will allow you to view a sample video for the Dr. Pepper Tuition Giveaway, which runs in the fall between September and December: www.youtube.com/watch?v=jybOmDhbJaw. The Dr. Pepper Tuition Giveaway is judged and voted on by the public; sort of like American Idol. The following link will allow you to view the details of the competition. www.drpeppertuition.com/?utm_campaign=drpepper&utm_source=aug21&utm_medium=email&utm_content=ENTER-TO-WIN.

My kids' school even played a part in shooting the scholarship video. Nicole's high school was in the process of installing solar panels on the roof. One Sunday we stopped by and asked the supervisor on site if we could go on top of the building and look at the project. To our surprise, he said yes. It probably helped that the supervisor spoke Spanish and we could too. I required all of my children to be bilingual so that they could communicate with more people.

Even though Nicole was scared of heights, she and her sister climbed the ladder and reached the rooftop. We were fascinated by the sea of solar panels on the roof. We had our cameras, hard hats and shot footage to include in the scholarship video. Even with all of that we still had not yet secured enough money to get a full ride.

Just when I resolved that I had to start looking for a second job, my daughter received a phone call with sensational news that made me run through the house shouting, "Thank you, Jesus!" It was a scholarship committee informing my daughter that she had a full tuition scholarship. This demonstrates how making a conscientious effort to groom your children for college and financing college through scholarships can become a reality. But remember, all of this starts with that competitive student profile.

So the lesson on this part of the trip is that it's hard work, but do the work, be patient and keep the faith. You won't be sorry.

A Competitive Student Profile– The Fuel that Propels the Full Academic Ride

How did we get to this place? My husband and I, with an empty nest, travel on fun get-a- ways now, and life is free from the stress of college expenses.

The competitive student profile we built is what propelled the trip to a full ride to college for our children. We started building their profiles early in their academic careers. We did not wait until senior year. Senior year is when you present your competitive student profile and let it do the work for you. It is not, however, when you start to build it. Everything should be in place by the end of junior year.

Nothing is more disheartening than when parents come to me seeking advice on college funding once their child hits senior year of high school. This type of thing is when the saying that "It's better late than never" could possibly be too late. Parents, we really want to start working on and building our children's student profile as soon as they enter middle school. How do we start? That's easy; start with the end in mind. I have an author friend, E. N. Joy, who always writes the ending of her books first. When I asked her why, she stated, "Because if you know what you want your ending to be, it's easier to take the steps required to get to that desired outcome." I find this to be true in life period. It's far less difficult to get somewhere when you know where you are going. So the student profile should reflect the student's ultimate higher education goals.

So you want to know just what is this competitive student profile I keep mentioning? Well, think of it as a résumé submitted by perspective faculty for a position at a university. Universities hire based on who they think will be successful in their disciplines and at educating the students. Likewise, colleges admit students they think will be able to excel in the classroom. They want students that have taken Advance Placement (AP) courses and have achieved AP test scores of three or more in those college level courses. It goes without saying that they are looking for students with good grades. Find out what the typical profile is for the students at the college you want to attend. Just visit the college's website. It will show you what you need in order to get offered a full ride scholarship from that university. Because, keep in mind, the number one scholarship you want to be sure the student applies for and is awarded is the all-inclusive scholarship offered by the school they will be attending.

College and scholarship committees are going to be most attracted to students that not only demonstrate they can handle the course load, but students that will add to the culture, experience and enrichment of the college campus and community. They want to give money to students that have demonstrated that they will be a good investment. So grades are not the only criteria. They are looking for students that have experience in community service and giving back, because they know that student is already programmed in philanthropy. The student profile should showcase such. Below is a breakdown of what a competitive student profile should reflect:

- Ranked in the top 3% of the students across the country
- National Honor Society Inductee
- Grade Point Average (GPA) of 3.8 - 4.2
- Transcript loaded with AP courses
- ACT score of 29 and above
- Superior writing and communication skills
- 100 hours of community service
- 10 letters of recommendation
- Prewritten essays
  (be prepared with the most commonly requested essays)
  -Biographical (1,000 words)
  -Why you want to major in your chosen field
  -What do you see yourself doing in 10, 20 or 30 years
- 2 years of participation in programs to demonstrate interest and aptitude in desired field
- Résumé
- A professional photo in hard copy and electronic form
- Professional attire for interviews and awards events

Components of the Competitive Student Profile

These are the components of a competitive student profile. To be honest, your student does not have to have all of the components listed, but this is what you should aim for. Now let's take a closer look at some of the components.

-Testing, Testing-One-Two-Testing; Getting a competitive ACT and SAT score

As mentioned earlier, the student's GPA at the end of their junior year is the GPA

colleges will see. If you are not satisfied with your ACT or SAT scores or if they are not competitive, you do have time to retake them and get a better score…if you study for them. Colleges and scholarship committees offer the best scholarships to students with ACT and SAT scores way above the national average. The national average is a 21 composite for the ACT and 516 Verbal and 501 Math for the SAT. So your scores need to be much higher than average to be competitive.

- ACT-register at www.ACT.org. It's around $37.00 without the writing test and $52.00 with the writing test (I strongly recommend including the writing)
- SAT-register at www.Collegeboard.org. It's around $51.00

If you qualify for free or reduced lunch at school, you can get a waiver from the school counselor to take the ACT or SAT free. But this is only good in senior year. Also, it will not cover late registration cost, so make sure you register on time.

This is crunch time! If your ACT and SAT score is not as high as you want it, use this time to study and increase your score. The higher your ACT and SAT scores, the greater the number of college admittances and more competitive scholarships you will qualify for, period!

If your scores are not competitive, hire a tutor. I recommend www.techtutorsonline.com; ACT and SAT preparation are their areas of expertise.

-Community service

Seek out volunteer opportunities helping the most destitute members in our society or assisting agencies and organizations that do. The places where people really need help are centers that serve low-income communities, hospice, homeless shelters, nursing homes or non-profit after school learning centers. To be competitive the student needs to rack up at least 100 plus hours of community service to add to the profile. Summer of rising junior year is the best time to accumulate those hours. The reason is because committees like to see your service within a twenty-four month time before receiving your application. So if you are already a senior and haven't done so, start on this immediately.

Remember to get letters of recommendation from the organizations. The letters should include how many hours were volunteered and specifics on how the student helped the beneficiaries of the organization. Community service should be one of the highlights in your essays, because the essence of a good essay is to explain how you will give back to the community or how you have already given back to the community. The colleges and scholarship committees are looking to give money to individuals who, in turn, will give back.

-Letters of recommendation

Ask for a letter of recommendation from your teachers, school counselors and community leaders way before the submission deadlines. People are busy and need time to fit another task into their schedules. Believe it or not, one of my children's teachers gave them the requested letter of recommendation on the last day of their senior year even though the letter was requested at the beginning of the school year. The teacher apologized for being overwhelmed and busy, which prevented her from getting the letter to my child sooner. Students have to be proactive. Send a thank you note even before the letter gets done. It is a great way to gently remind them.

Secure at least ten letters of recommendation to have on hand, i.e. two from math teachers, two from Language Arts teachers, and one from the counselor. And don't forget the letters for the community service that was performed. The student may ask for ten letters but only receive eight or nine. Having an assortment to choose from gives the student the opportunity to choose the most appropriate and well written letters for a particular college and/or scholarship.

I would be remiss if I did not talk about how important manners and getting along with people are in regards to letters of recommendation. Letters of recommendation are the best way for scholarship committees to judge the character of the applicant. Therefore, what is stated about the student in the letter can make or break their chances of being awarded funds. Generally, it is protocol for a letter of recommendation to be sent directly to the school counselors without the student's review. Consequently, make sure the person writing the letter is asked if they can write a positive letter of recommendation. The student may have a great relationship with the teacher, but what if they had a bad review about behavior from a substitute teacher-like me?

I would also be negligent if I did not mention that students should not post vulgar, inappropriate, slanderous or any other thing that will diminish their character on social media. The digital footprint is never really erased; it is out there on someone's computer and on the server computer that transmitted the image or information. In fact, I did a Google search for my daughter's name and I was amazed at what came up. Most of the scholarships she was awarded and many of her post on twitter were revealed. Social media is public information!

Colleges and scholarship committees do look at Facebook and other social media streams, and the information can be found by a simple Google search of your name.

Students should have on their best manners at all times and understand that their character is based on how they act when they think no one is looking. Because trust me; someone is always looking!

-Essays–Write your way to thousands of dollars

Anticipate the following types of essays for college and scholarship applications and have your student prepared by prewriting essays over the summer. Essays should always demonstrate and give examples of how the student is giving back to the community and their eagerness to continue to give back.

- Biographical
- Chosen field of study
- 10, 20, even 30 year life projection (what will the student be doing in 10, 20, 30 years from now?)

Think of the college essay as a face-to-face interview. The student should tell them why they are the best candidate. This is not the time to be modest; it is a golden opportunity to make an unforgettable impression. Make sure your personality comes across in the written essay. Make it personal, interesting, unique and engaging, and most of all make sure it has been edited for grammar several times. This is why I suggest a student taking no more than five classes senior year. They need time during the day to write award winning essays and have them edited.

The student should not let anybody else write their essays for them. The essays should be the student's own thoughts and ideas. Why? Because when they are called for an interview due to making the top five candidates, they may be asked a question from their essay that requires profound knowledge of the topic of the essay. If the student fumbles and cannot give a coherent answer, the committee may think the student did not write it, forfeiting the chances of being awarded the scholarship. I elaborate more on scholarship interviews in the scholarships section, so make sure you read that section.

Students should use the resources at their school; go to the writing lab to get help with essays. If there is no writing lab, go to the Language Arts department and ask one of the teachers to review the essays or you can submit it to FreeRidetocollege.com/services for help. We offer additional services on our website that are available for a modest fee. Just fill out and submit the request form on the website. Some of the services available are listed below:

- Portfolio/Profile Assistance- we will review the student profile and offer suggestions on how to improve it with presentation and content
- Essay Writing Coaching, Evaluation and Review
- Essay Editing Services
- Tutoring Referral for Academic and ACT Improvement

-Résumé

Your résumé should emphasize your high school honors, awards and accomplishments. Have a list of people and their contact information you have asked to give you a positive reference in case any committee wants to call them. Let your references know you are listing them so they won't be caught off guard when the calls come and they are not prepared to respond. Ask them what is the best way for a scholarship committee to contact them, then provide that information on the résumé or application.

Students Take the Wheel – It's Your Responsibility Too

Students, picture yourself in your senior year. You're getting phone calls, letters and even plane tickets to visit colleges and universities. Now that's what I call ballin' out! That is a true baller; being courted by higher education institutions. Athletes are not the only ones that are recruited heavily. Colleges and universities recruit the best and brightest in the same manner they recruit athletes.

Have you ever said, "I can't wait until I'm eighteen, so I can leave?" If I had a dime for every time my children made that comment, well, I wouldn't have to worry about securing college money for them. When they voiced such, I didn't get mad. I just thought to myself, I am going to make sure that when you are ready to leave, you ride out in style, with a full ride and money in the bank-but not my money!

With this mentality to counter my children's, those that have already spread their wings did so not only with full rides to college, but with other offers of monthly stipends of seven hundred fifty dollars to nine hundred dollars as well. They actually turned down those other offers, but it was a nice option. One offer was made by a very prestigious university, but it did not have all the bells and whistles of college life, such as a division one football team. It was small and not in a city they wanted to live in.

I was determined that my children would be prepared for and not have to struggle through college…and that neither would I in trying to pay for it. So to all the students entering high school; if you start counting down the days until you leave, you will find that you don't have much time, so get to test driving those wings!

You have to have your student profile in optimal presentation by the end of your junior year. Since you will apply to college after your junior year, colleges will not see your senior year grades until after you have been admitted. But beware; your counselor is required to send your final grades to the college and the college has the right to rescind any admission of a student that did not perform to standard their senior year. Therefore, your major countdown to being college ready stops at the end of junior year, but the clock doesn't stop ticking senior year.

-Choosing a college-Time for the stop at the information center –College Fairs

College fairs are the most economical way to get students connected with college admissions representatives. The fairs typically begin in September of every school year.

Below are links to college fairs in central Ohio, where I live, that I used for my own children. But with the click of your mouse, you can search the internet for college fairs in your neck of the woods.

www.college-fair.org/
www.ohiohbcucollegefair.com/

www.bexleyareacollegefair.com/columbus.html
www.granvilleschools.org/CollegeFairsinCentralOhio.
aspx

Additionally, colleges schedule visits to high schools throughout the year. They also hold mini college information sessions at local hotel meeting rooms. Check with your high school guidance office for additional times and locations of college fairs, college representatives visiting the school and mini college fairs at local venues.

Community colleges should get a look too. They are much less expensive and have wonderful scholarships available for competitive students. They also have programs to get your student trained and working within twenty-four months.

-College visits

During senior year there is just not enough time, and often money, to visit every college your child is interested in. Make your va-cations "edu-cations" by planning college visits along the way every time you and your family visit a new city or state over the years. At the least, during sophomore and junior year of high school, you should visit the top choices of colleges the student wants to attend. Aim to visit the campus during the semester in order to get a comprehensive view of the college. This way, you can talk to students that attend the university and get a more objective view of the college.

Make it fun for your student; take some of their friends along. I always loaded up my car with as many students as I could fit and took them with us. The trips were usually no more than a four hour drive to the university. To maximize your time, review your student's school's academic calendar and important dates and schedule your visits around the days they have breaks from high school. If you are concerned about racking up unexcused absences during your senior year, don't be. High school's grant their seniors and juniors at least three excused, planned absences for college visits.

Now that you know you have the luxury of planning your college visits during the semester, call the university to set up a visit. Most universities have a schedule for the college tours. You can call the Admissions Office to schedule your appointment. Or even better, call the department the student will matriculate in and find a point person. For instance, if the student wants to major in business, call that department and talk to their recruiter. They will be happy to accommodate you.

I have been on many group visits on campuses, and I have been on many private visits. It was not uncommon for my kids to be invited for a visit and get the royal treatment just like an athlete. The universities had a private lunch set up for us with key people from the engineering department joining us as well as current students to answer any questions we had. On the larger campuses, they also arranged for a chauffer to drive us around the campus. If you have any questions or requests, just ask. Most colleges are very resourceful when they are trying to attract new students.

When you visit a college, take note of the living quarters. Are there adequate dorms for incoming students on campus? Although the student probably won't spend a lot of time there, other than sleeping, make sure it is comfortable. It is also a good idea to grab a bite at the campus eatery. The Admissions Office usually gives out vouchers for meals, or at least a discount coupon, for perspective students. Make sure they have healthy choices and the food tastes good. You have heard about the freshman fifteen, right? That is the average number of pounds a college freshman gains. So, healthy food choices are an important consideration.

Just as important as diet is exercise, so take note of how conducive the environment is for exercising. Look for walking trails, exercise facilities, bike racks, etc… on campus. Exercising, keeping fit and not gaining weight will also help with self esteem, energy level, and relieves stress for busy students. Besides, it will keep the student from having to buy an expensive new wardrobe because they can no longer fit all the clothes purchased in preparation of going off to college. Students need to keep the brain functioning optimally. Physical exercise not only keeps the body healthy, but the brain as well, because the brain uses twenty percent of the body's oxygen. Those are some of the important considerations for college. Now for the big decision; where to go to college.

-Fork in the road: To which college do I go?

One of the most important considerations when choosing a college is does the school have the intended major and how is it ranked in that discipline. Equally as important is whether the school is accredited by a regional college accreditation association. Accreditation assures that the college meets certain standards for a quality education. The primary reasons you want to make sure your college is accredited is that if it is not, there are no government grants or loans available. You can get private loans, but they are generally at a much higher interest rate and have less flexible terms when it comes time to pay them back. The student's credits may not transfer to other colleges if that need arises. Also, if the school is not accredited, their degree may not be recognized by certain employers.

It is easy to find the top school in the student's desired field. For instance, if the student wants to major in nursing and wants to know what the best schools in nursing are, Google or Bing search for "top colleges for undergraduate nursing programs." Or you can find out by visiting the following link: www.america.edu/top_20_nursing_programs_in_america.htm.

Do you prefer the hustle and bustle of the city or the laid back atmosphere of the country? Cities have more things to do outside of college, which can translate into more distractions. Or it could translate into more opportunities to give back, network and work as an intern while attending college. Keep in mind that having a college degree plus work experience makes the student more marketable when the job search starts after college. Cities also have more food choices and eateries that stay open late to accommodate various schedules. Rural schools have fewer distractions, so the student can focus better, which may translate in to your student graduating in the customary four years? But there are not as many things to do outside of student life without traveling some distance.

"You can make a big school smaller, but you cannot make a small school bigger." That is what my kids reasoned when they chose big universities to attend. But choose a big or small campus based on your own comfort level.

The pros of smaller campuses are the smaller class sizes. A smaller class size means more access to the professor and a more proverbial relationship with your professors. I can tell you from an educator's standpoint that there is less stress with fewer students, so the professors tend to be more personable. The smaller campus tends to have more of a family environment with students and faculty also.

The cons of a smaller campus are that they appear less competitive. Some are not as well-known and tend to usually be more expensive.

The pros of the larger campuses is that they usually have more resources such as work study programs, tutors, a variety of places to eat and workout facilities just to name a few. The cons of a bigger campus ranges from the fact that many students get lost and are not able to navigate socially or academically, to the fact that bigger schools also have a much more competitive, cut throat academic environment.

From a financial aspect, there is a huge difference between private and public colleges. Private colleges are very expensive. However, don't let the high price tag deter you from applying. Did you know that Harvard University is one of the most affordable universities depending on how you look at it? Harvard and other Ivy League schools don't give merit based scholarships; it's all based on financial need. If you get into Harvard and your family income is less than sixty thousand dollars a year, you qualify for a full need based scholarship! They also give aid to families with incomes over sixty thousand dollars on a sliding scale. Many private schools will put together a working financial package to help students.

Private colleges other than the Ivy League also have resources through endowments to meet the financial needs of students they really have an interest in. I have found that if they want you, they will find money for a student with an impressive profile.

Private schools also have a nurturing quality about them and they tend to be small. What do I mean by nurturing? Once we were on a visit to a small, private, prestigious college. While we were in the dean's office, he mentioned that right before we came into his office he was about to make a call and find out why a student missed class.

That's like getting a call from your mom checking on you, I thought. Could that ever happen at a big school? Maybe it was just for show, but I liked the fact that they were concerned about the student. I really wanted my child to attend that college but they did not like the campus. Since I am not the one that has to do the work and live on campus, I allowed my kids to my make their own decision when it came to their choice of college.

Public universities are supplemented financially by tax dollars from their state, so they are not as expensive as private schools. They generally have lots of scholarships available to attract the top students. Having such a huge alumni base gives their endowment funds lots of resources to offer competitive students full rides. State universities also offer students with state residency lower tuition rates.

There are many other things to consider, such as athletic programs, and that goes for whether the student plans on participating or spectating. Are there professors or graduate students teaching the classes? What is the professor to student ratio and the reputation of the school?

To narrow down your choice, you should consider the previous details. You should also heavily consider any offers you have received in writing from colleges courting you. Narrow your choices down to about four colleges, because unless you have obtained a letter from your top desired college indicating that it intends to give you a full ride, you will have to fill out an application for each school. This means you will have to spend about fifty dollars per application.

On the Road Again- Applying to College

As far as actually applying to colleges, do not procrastinate on this! Don't let the lack of money stop you from applying to college. If you are on the free or reduced lunch plan at school, you qualify for a fee wavier on up to four college applications. The school counselors have these waivers. It's never too early to begin to make that connection and form a rapport with colleges. Let 'em know you're coming (or at least thinking about it anyway). Check the college website to verify the dates of early decision, early action and regular admissions.

If you really want to attend a certain college, apply through the early decision process. It increases your chances. Students should apply to colleges as early as possible. When I say early, I mean by August of the year prior to the desired admission. Visit the website of your desired college, note early decision dates, list the required documents for admission and begin working on them. At the least, have everything in place by the time you sit down to Thanksgiving dinner senior year.

Many colleges still have individual applications, but the use of the Common Application by universities has become more widespread. The Common Application has made getting into college a much more competitive feat.

What is the Common Application? It is where you fill out one application and you can easily submit it to up to 517 colleges and universities (www.commonapp.org).

Keep in mind that you are still required to pay a separate fee for each school and you are required to submit supplemental materials such as essays and letters of recommendation for each school as well.

Another consequence is, due to the larger number of applicants, the Common Application has made college admission and university sponsored scholarships much more competitive.

The ease of applying has increased the applicant pool tremendously. For example, prior to the Common Application, The Ohio State University had an average of 26,000 applicants. They joined the Common Application and in the fall of 2012 they had nearly 40,000 applications. That is why students need to apply early and file for their FAFSA early; competition!

Make Sure You Have Enough Gas – Required High School Graduation Credits

Before you hop in the car and head down the road that leads to college, make sure you have enough gas. By this I mean high school graduation credits. Most will agree that technically, in the average family, paving the way to college begins freshmen year of high school. I personally found that you have to start long before freshman year, more like sixth grade, especially now that the Common Core Educational Model is in effect in 45 out of the 50 states across the United States. Common Core requires students to have four years of math and pass Algebra 2 in order to graduate from high school. The Common Core standard of education is based on the premise that students should graduate with higher proficiencies in math and English. This was implemented in response to universities and employers declaring that American students lack adequate math and writing skills upon graduation from high school.

In addition, the Common Core synchronizes the curriculums of secondary schools across the country. One of the benefits is that no matter where your student is learning, your student is learning the same material other students in another state is learning. Consequently, if you have to pack up and move to another state in the middle of the school year, your child will not miss a beat. The continuity in learning will be the same.

Common Core also raises the standards for writing in the classrooms. As I indicated previously, colleges have said that students are coming to college without the ability to write fluently and employers are complaining that American students cannot communicate adequately in writing. Thus, there has been an increase in the number of students taking remedial classes in college before they can even start their college courses. For parents, this translates into a higher cost to educate your college student, because parents will have to pay for the remedial courses, and then pay for the core college courses after the student has been brought up to standard.

This means the most competitive students will take high school Algebra in middle school. It also means if you wait until high school to get serious about math and writing, your child will be at a huge disadvantage.

Since colleges evaluate students on their freshman, sophomore and junior years of high school, your student should already be groomed for success and competitive by the end of middle school. When the student starts high school, they should be on automatic pilot, in other words, already developed superior work ethics in the classroom, study habits at home and is self-disciplined and motivated. Your student should enter into ninth grade making the top grades. The fact is that it is harder to increase a low grade point average than it is to bring down a high one. Students that are the most competitive come into ninth grade making the highest grades from the start of high school. After that, your scenic route through college town has an estimated time of thirty-six months left. Believe it or not, that is really not much time.

By senior year, your student should have already obtained all the credits needed to get a high school diploma. At worst, the student should only be shy of maybe one or two credits that they have to take. I never allowed my children to take more than five classes senior year. Even though my kids all graduated with 28 to 29 credits from high school (significantly higher than the required 20 for the state of Ohio, which was recently raised to 21 by Common Core), senior year they only took the required five classes. This allowed them to get early release from school, and that gave them the time needed to research, apply to and write the essays for the scholarships.

Knowing where the student stands every step of their high school career in regards to their high school requirements is crucial. The high school counselor is the best person to let students know where they stand. As a parent and student, you can request a meeting with the school counselor in order to know the right classes to take in order to accelerate your student's progress.

The student can take their required physical education, health and other classes in the summer to ease the load during the regular school year. Some schools even give physical education credits for participation in high school sports. Another option is the student can forgo having a study center or a lunch period. I know; it sounds a little bit over the top, but these are just some of the sacrifices my kids made to have reduced classes senior year to make sure they had time to apply for scholarships.

So now you can see why your child needs to be over prepared for high school; because you only have 36 months that zoom by. All of my children were aggressively knocking out the required credits in the first 36 months of high school, all while participating in football, wrestling, concert band, marching band, cross country, international language club, just to name a few. In addition, they attended Saturday School to give them an edge. I will elaborate on the benefits of Saturday School as well as sports, band, choir, national honor society and other extracurricular activities and honors in future volumes. Inevitably, all my children ended up with some crazy out of sorts schedule before senior year in order to make sure they ended up having no more than those five classes to take.

As you can see, building the perfect situation with the high school credit does not take on the typical form. It takes lots of planning to achieve. Students should meet with their high school counselor yearly to make sure that they are on the right track. For those parents that want to look at the high school graduation requirements for your state, visit www.education.(your state).gov and put "graduation requirements" in the search box.

The bottom line is that you should partner with your

child's high school counselor to stay on the right path. You will be happy you did when all the senior matters come up, because senior year you will not only be deciding on colleges, but considering the following as well:

- Applying to college
- College visits
- Deciding which college to attend
- Applying for scholarships
- Homecoming and prom attire
- Senior pictures
- Cap and gown orders
- Order and sending out graduation announcements
- Attending awards events to honor your student's accomplishments
- Scholarship interviews
- Planning the graduation party or open house
- Extra curricular activity commitments
- Attending the programs to receive the scholarships

Senior Prom is a major senior year event!

One of the highlights of senior year is prom. Having only five classes is helpful in preparing. There are hours of shopping for the right attire, deciding on a date, hair, nails, transportation, dinner, the prom itself and the after party. It is a big and important day to your student that they have surely earned!

As you can see, senior year is expensive and can be overwhelming, so do yourself a favor and try to make your load as light as possible. Within those five senior classes your student will take, I recommend the student not take more than two really challenging classes such as Advance Placement classes. Senior year is a very stressful year for both parents and students. Prepare and plan to reduce the stress.

My daughter, Nicole, hit a huge brick wall senior year. She became overwhelmed with what seemed to be hyper-insomnia and could not sleep. It was not an easy fix. She went to several doctors and had two sleep studies, and the doctors still could not figure out what was wrong. Not being able to sleep adversely affected her mood, energy level and concentration. So in addition to dealing with the pressure of senior year, she could not sleep well. It was horrifying. My child was tired all the time and could hardly function with all the senior business to take care of. Needless to say, her grades did suffer some, but having a high enough GPA going into senior year, the university did not rescind her acceptance. Anything can happen, so make sure your student is prepared as far in advance as possible. Prepared for what? EVERY and ANYTHING!

Getting a Jump Start on College Cost by Earning College Credits in High School

There are several ways to reduce the cost of college while in high school and make your student a more competitive candidate for college. The two most popular ways to accomplish this is through Advance Placement courses and postsecondary options while in high school. My son Carlos graduated from high school with enough college credits to be classified as a sophomore in college. Translation: If I would have had to pay for his college tuition, it would have only been for three years, which is a savings anywhere from twenty-three to sixty thousand dollars depending on where your student ends up going to college. I will deal with this subject in depth in the volume that will focus on the sophomore year.

If your student waits until senior year to take AP classes, the universities will not have the benefit of seeing what grade your student will get prior to determining your student's acceptance or not. Colleges don't see the senior year grades until after the student has been admitted, so it has no bearing on helping the admissions committee decide that this student can truly handle college level work. But if your student has taken Advance Placement prior to senior year and earned at least a three or better on the test, your student will get college credit and it will help the admissions committee determine the student's ability to perform in college.

Although not as wide spread, the International Baccalaureate Program (IB), is another way to earn college credit in high school. There are also programs that give high school students the opportunity to take college courses on a college campus while in high school. This option gives the student an edge and has huge benefits, but there are some important issues to consider. I discuss this and IB in the sophomore year volume.

When it's Okay to Put the Cart Before the Horse-Start Your Scholarship Search Early

Applying for college scholarships may seem like putting the cart before the horse when the student hasn't even been accepted to college, but that's quite all right. Scholarship season runs between August of rising senior year to about April of senior year, with the bulk of them being between December and late March. Being prepared to submit the scholarship applications is the most important aspect of applying. The list of profile items that I gave you earlier apply to both college applications and scholarship applications alike.

It is imperative that these documents are ready to go during scholarship season. You will be searching and applying for scholarships for high school graduating seniors. The most advantageous situation is to pre-search and catalog, during junior year, the scholarships you will qualify for that upcoming senior year. This will give you an idea of what is available in scholarships and exactly what you will need in order to attain money in your chosen field of study. Some scholarships will allow you to sign up for electronic updates via your email address. In turn, they will send you an email notice when the scholarship opens the next year. Some scholarships will fall off the map and no longer be available the next year primarily because of lack of funding. Nevertheless, it is imperative to have the following things in place to greater assist in securing funding:

- Ranked in the top 3% of the students across the country
- GPA of 3.8 - 4.2
- Transcript loaded with AP courses
- ACT and SAT scores significantly above national average
- Superior writing and communication skills
- 100 hours of community service
- 10 letters of recommendation

- o Prewritten essays (be prepared with the most commonly requested essays)
  -Biographical (1,000 words)
  -Why you want to major in your chosen field
  -What do you see yourself doing in 10, 20 or 30 years
- o 2 years of participation in programs to demonstrate interest and aptitude in desired field
- o Résumé
- o A professional photo in hard copy and electronic form
- o Professional attire for interviews and awards events

When applying for scholarships you probably won't be totally sure where you are going to attend college, but again, that's okay. After you have been awarded the scholarship, you will have the opportunity to let the scholarship committee know.

Organizing the scholarships is another very important aspect of successfully securing them. You can use a notebook, files or whatever system you use to keep things in order. I used Microsoft Word to make a chart or table. See an example below:

Due date	Required documents	Name of scholarship	Amount
Enter a date 2 weeks earlier than the actual due date	It is very important to make sure you have all required documents- Missing documents will disqualify the applicant	Put the hyperlink to the scholarship here	$300, $500, $1,000, $100,000, etc…

I eventually color coded the items based on what was submitted, awarded or denied.

This system of organization helped me, at-a-glance, to keep track of the awards. Also, please note that the due date is the most important thing you want to document. Missing deadlines could mean missing out on money. If you happen to miss a deadline, just check the scholarship website. I have seen them extend the deadline many times, especially when a natural disaster has occurred in the United States. But don't rely on that; submit your scholarship applications no later than a week earlier than the deadline if you can. If you wait until the last minute, there is a good chance the server will be overwhelmed and will not accept your application, which has happened to me only once. But it taught me a lesson to always try to submit early. And last, but certainly not least, don't forget to hand write and send 'thank you' letters to the scholarship committees…for the ones you were awarded of course.

Show Me the Money-
The Scholarship Search

When I first started applying for scholarships with my kids, I tried to apply for every scholarship out there. I was just spinning my wheels. I don't want you to waste your time doing that. Your time is valuable, so investigate and give careful consideration to the type of scholarships you qualify for. Look at your current profile and establish what scholarships you have the best chance of getting. I found out the hard way that my family did not qualify for many of the need based scholarships. Of course I found this out after investing all my time and energy into applying for them.

There are three main types of scholarships available to students: Merit Based, Community Service Based and Need Based Scholarships. Merit Based University Scholarships are one of the best types of scholarships to have because they make college life easy by eliminating the need to go to the bursar's office. When it comes time to register for classes and pay your tuition, there is really nothing for the student or the parent to worry about. The university credits the student's account with thousands of dollars. There is no paperwork, waiting or explanations and no keeping track of payments.

Merit Based University Scholarships are extremely competitive. They are looking for the best and the brightest, and, once again, the most competitive student profiles. You might have heard, "To whom much is given much is expected." Keep that in mind, because they expect a lot if you are going to get their money.

If you have served your community one hundred hours or more, you are a good candidate for Community Service Based Scholarships. The good thing about Community Service Based Scholarships is the scholarship committee is not so much concerned with the student's income, GPA or ACT scores. They just want to know about the student's service to the community.

When the student performs community service, it is a good idea to keep a journal/log of the specifics about who in the organization was helped, how the student helped the organization as well as how the organization benefited from the service. This will make a great reference when writing essays and highlighting the student's philanthropy.

Remember to have letters of recommendation from an officer of the community service organization ready with details about your service. Community Service Based Scholarships like to see students help the most deprived members of society.

Essays for Community Service Based Scholarship should tell about the wonderful and helpful things the student has done for the community. Describe the persons or organization that you helped and how you helped them in detail. Give examples. Paint the picture so that they can visualize the situation and how you helped.

The essay should always be your own thoughts and must be accurate. Community Service Based Scholarships are the most likely ones where the scholarship committee does their due diligence and verifies everything you put in the essay. These scholarships, once awarded, are often sent directly to the student in the form of a check if it is a national scholarship. If it is a local scholarship, the organization usually has some kind of event to highlight your charity and will not always, but most of the time, give you the check at the event. Otherwise, they will send it to the college the student attends and the college in turn credits it to the student's account.

To qualify for most Need Based Scholarships, which are scholarships for economically disadvantaged students, the student will have to show their Estimated Family Contribution Number from their Free Application for Federal Student Aid.

Although this publication is about full academic rides, I want to include a few words about athletic scholarships. One of my kids found themself in a precarious situation; being offered both full academic and athletic scholarships. So which is best? First of all, please note that all athletes that receive scholarship offers have to go through the National Collegiate Athletic Association (NCAA) Clearing House to qualify. You can find details by visiting the NCAA website. You should also talk to your counselor to make sure your student meets the eligibility requirements. Also note that once you are awarded an athletic scholarship, you are limited on the amount of additional money you can receive for college. My child had to end up giving back some of the scholarship money awarded because of those limits. The good news is that there is no limit to how much money a student can receive for academic scholarships.

You might recall my mentioning earlier the video scholarship my daughter did for Dr. Pepper, well there are an endless number of corporate scholarships. Remember, every corporation has a foundation. Look for scholarships on the corporate responsibility link of the business' website or do a search for scholarships or philanthropy on the business' website.

Scholarships for Performing and Visual Arts Students

If you are one of those gifted performing or visual art students, there are many scholarships and competitions for you to win money as well. Performing and visual arts schools are looking for the most talented students and they have money for the most competitive students. To showcase the scope and depth of your talent, Visual Arts students should start a portfolio of their work as early in their school career as possible. Likewise, Performing Arts students should prepare a repertory of their best dialogues or music selections for auditions to performing arts schools. Once the student has been scheduled for an audition, double check the time and place, and by all means be over prepared and on time. You can do a Google search for performing and visual arts college fairs to find one in your area.

Grants and Federal Loans VS. Private Loans

In order to qualify for government grants and loans, you must fill out a FAFSA. Pell grants and loans are set aside by the federal government to help even the playing field for students from lower income families. The grants are just that, grants; you don't have to pay them back. Grant money is distributed by the university on a first come first serve bases. So do not delay your application; be the first to apply!

Make sure your parents file their federal income tax and your FAFSA as soon as it is available, especially for state supported public universities. Funds are limited. Private universities operate a little differently. If they accept you, generally they are going to do everything they can to help you cover your college expenses. Remember, they have endowment funds for the students they select. So never dismiss a college because of cost. They do have resources waiting to use on you.

Private loans are also available, but with much higher interest rates and less flexible terms. Most banks and credit card companies have student loan programs. You can also check with Sallie Mae, which is the largest student loan bank in the United States. But be careful with student loans. Always borrow responsibly, because you do have to pay the money back soon after graduating. Even with the student loan forgiveness programs, I have talked to many college graduates that wish they had worked more while in college, so they would have a lower student loan debt.

When it comes to Need Based Scholarships being distributed, again, I can't express enough how important it is for parents to file the FAFSA as soon as it becomes available, because need based money is distributed on a first come first serve bases. Hence; file your income taxes as early as possible to get the most accurate evaluation for funds. You can file the

FAFSA before filing your taxes, but the amount of aid awarded could change based on the tax return.

The money from Need Based Scholarships often, but not always, goes directly to the college, and unfortunately, the amount of aid you get from the government may be reduced. This happens because any money you get from an outside scholarship is considered income.

Merit Based Scholarships are based on the student's academic profile. To qualify for Merit Based Scholarships, they usually want the whole package; top 5-10% of the senior class. So know where the student ranks. They also consider the student's GPA; 3.0 - 4.2 is the range the student will want to aim for. They will consider how many AP courses the student took as well as ACT and SAT scores.

Recently, colleges have put more emphasis on being college ready by putting more weight on one's writing skills. Consequently, they give strong consideration to writing scores on the ACT. So to be competitive, always include the writing portion on your ACT test.

Merit Based Scholarships usually require several essays. I have seen some that require up to thirteen essays. They also look at community service, letters of recommendation, lots of constructive extracurricular activities and a résumé.

Your primary source of scholarships should be local scholarships or scholarships that are only available to students in your city or school. High School counselors get scholarship information weekly. Check with the guidance office at least once a week. While you are there, be extra nice to your counselor and the secretary. You are going to need them to be on call when you need a last minute letter of recommendation sent electronically or a transcript sent to a college or scholarship committee...although your letters of recommendation should already be complete and in their possession. Remember, you should have asked for the letters in writing before the first day of school senior year.

You should have an electronic and hard copy of official and non-official transcripts on hand in case you run into a last minute scholarship opportunity. One last but very important place to check for scholarships is the financial aid page of the website for your prospective college. It will have the scholarships that students enrolled at that university qualify for.

The Road Less Traveled-Unconventional College Funding

Do you have a student prodigy? Well that is money in the bank too. My kids participated in the arts at school. They spent years in solo and ensemble, and I paid for private music lessons. Although none of them are going to be famous musicians, they do have some marketable talent, which has won them many talent contests. It's just more money in the bank.

-Talent competitions

There are all kinds of talent competitions for scholarship money. If your student has participated in arts at school, they will have a chance to use it. In Columbus, Ohio the Mu Iota Chapter of Omega Psi Phi Fraternity has a Talent Hunt Program. The top three winners take home a cash prize of $1,000, $750 and $500, respectively.

-Essay contests

Essay contests can be easy ways to acquire money. Usually this type of competition is not concerned with any aspect of the student profile except verifying certain information with your school counselor. All you have to do is write an award winning essay. The other plus is that they usually send the check directly to the student after verifying the student's status with the guidance counselor.

-Make your graduation party a college fundraiser

I am not fond of the traditional graduation announcements; you know the cards with the school logo and the boring smaller card with the name on it that always gets misplaced, and then you have to add a wallet size picture and stuff it all in an envelope? Ugh! That is so old fashion, and besides, who carries photos in their wallets anymore? We have smart-phones now to show off pictures.

Instead of buying the traditional announcements, I created a postcard with a keepsake 'then and now' type of picture of my daughter. It had a picture of her when she was in elementary school and a current picture. Everybody loved it! They would look at it and express how they remembered her as a child and comment that she has really grown up. I had the printer make 1,000 copies and we sent out about 500. It was even cheaper to mail them out versus the traditional announcements because they were postcards. Now, every time I visit someone who received one, they have it visibly displayed in their home and not buried in their wallet. I invested about five hundred dollars in her graduation party, a yard banner and my unique announcements. From that investment she received over four thousand dollars in gifts.

People will help fund an education; you just have to send them an announcement and invitation to the graduation celebration/open house. If they cannot attend, most will send a gift for congratulations...especially if you send a really nice keepsake picture!

This Scholarship Is For You: Where to Find Scholarships Your Student Qualifies For

The number one place you should look for scholarships your student qualifies for is www.naviance.com. This valuable website posts specific scholarships for your particular school. You will need a user name and password, which you can get from your school counselor. If your school does not subscribe to Naviance.com, find a friend whose school does and ask him/her to share the information with you.

An equally important resource is your school counselor and secretary. They are usually aware of all local scholarships that come into the guidance office. The next important resource is the website of the local foundation for your city, county or state. For example, in Columbus, Ohio most residents will qualify for some of the scholarships on The Columbus Foundation's website, which is www.columbusfoundation.com. Your church, employer, sorority, fraternity and community newsletters are the next source for scholarships for the student. Ask everybody you know about the organizations they are involved with and any scholarships the organization sponsors.

Your scholarship search should begin with:

-Local scholarships

- www.naviance.com
- School counselor
- Local foundations
- Community newsletters
- Church
- Employer
- Sororities and Fraternities

-National scholarships

The national scholarship list is endless and more competitive, so choose wisely because your time is valuable during this process. I have listed the resources below:

www.studentscholarships.org
www.fastweb.com
www.scholarships.com
www.scholarshipsonline.org
www.ScholarshipAmerica.com

Fastweb.com, Scholarships.com and other national list will require you to set up an account, followed by a questionnaire interview to narrow down the scholarships in which the student qualifies. It will take some time to answer the questions, but it is worth it. After filling out the interview questions, they will e-mail the scholarships you qualify for to your inbox. This is why you need to have the profile documents ready to go; so that you will have mostly everything ready for the opportunities that you will be offered.

One of the best places to look for and submit scholarships is through electronic sources. They are easy to submit because they don't get lost in the mail. Do specific scholarship searches in Google. For example:

- Scholarships for single moms
- Scholarships for red heads
- Scholarships for males majoring in education
- Scholarships for veterans
- Scholarships for children of veterans
- Scholarship for women in engineering
- Scholarships for males in nursing

You will find more than enough scholarships if you apply specific information through your searches. Remember to search for specific scholarships for a specific major. UNDECIDED is not a major. If you are not finding scholarships for your intended major, this may indicate the demand for your field of study is low. Society invests money in fields that are in demand. Just as when in 1961 President Kennedy launched the RACE to the Moon project; it was a race to educate engineers. Today there is a race for innovation. So the type of majors that will have a great deal of available money will be those related to Science, Technology, Engineering and Math (STEM). The other alternative is to be ranked in the top three percent of the students academically and you can major in anything you want because you will get the university scholarships for the top academic students.

-The Scholarship interview

Congratulations, you are a semi-finalist. Even with a stellar profile, sometimes it comes down to the interview, so be prepared. The scholarship interview is your opportunity to impress the scholarship committee. Be well versed in your field. This moment is why parents should encourage children to speak up for themselves and learn to communicate effectively with people in positions of authority. We have got to let go of some (not all) of the old fashion ways of raising our children. For example, have you ever heard this: "Speak only when you're spoken to," or, "Come when you are called?" How are your kids supposed to be self-advocates if they cannot speak up for themselves and get practice around their parents? Communicating effectively, yet respectively, with authority is a very important skill that can help get one ahead. Teach your child to speak up for himself, to communicate with the doctor for himself, to communicate with the preacher, teacher and principal. Let them practice and learn the art of communication. They are not being disrespectful just because they had an opinion or speak up for themselves.

Here are some tips for the interview:

- Be on time-arrive 15 minutes early
- Dress professionally

- Put on your best smile, manners and make eye contact
- Review your essay for that scholarship; the committee will often ask questions from your essay
- Have a question prepared for the interviewer
- Practice with family

The Commencement of Your Journey-How Much Will it Cost to Send Your Child to College?

When I was raised in the engineering Mecca-Flint, Michigan in the 60's and 70's-if you were admitted to the prestigious General Motors Institute (GMI) engineering university, it was absolutely free to attend. Since then the name has been changed to Kettering University after a prominent General Motors Engineer and native Ohioan, Charles Franklin Kettering. To go along with the new name is a hefty new price tag. It has gone from free to $21,000 a year to attend the university. However, I matriculated at Howard University during the late 70's and early 80's and attained a degree in Microbiology. It cost my parents about five thousand dollars a year for tuition, room and board. Comparing those tuition fees to the cost of education today can leave any parent feeling anxious. A college education at Howard University is currently a staggering forty-one thousand dollars a year.

One of my siblings attended the University of Michigan in the 1980's and it cost about four thousand dollars a year. The cost of this university has skyrocketed to over $53,000 a year for an out of state student. Some universities are even at the $60,000 a year mark. Multiply that by four and it's a quarter of a million dollars to attain a four year degree. To calculate today's projected college for your future college tuition visit www.collegecost.ed.gov/catc/#.

Despite these costs, I was determined that all of my children would go to college. Not only would they go to college, but they would go with no out of pocket expense on the family's behalf. Sounds impossible, right? But I'd made up my mind that I would see to it that both myself and my children would do everything we possibly could to make the impossible a genuine possibility.

As parents, once we make up our minds about something in regards to our children, especially their education, we set out on an unstoppable mission, and that even includes a mission impossible. And so began my expedition to see to it that my children received a free ride to college. Do you have a challenge that seems impossible too? I hope you will allow me to guide you down some of the same roads and paths I took to bring my goals into fruition.

I cannot guarantee that your results will be identical to mine. What worked for me might not work for you or it could ultimately work even better for you. It just takes hard work, dedication and a whole lot of faith. It's understanding the quote by my editor, Joylynn M. Ross: "There is a big difference between doing the best that you can do and doing all that you can do." So put on your seatbelt. This ride is really just getting started.

A Call to Action

PARENTS, our children's education is our responsibility. We can tell our children all day every day that it is their responsibility to go to school, pay attention in class and to learn and absorb all their instructors set out to teach them. And that is true. But as parents, it is our responsibility to make sure this gets done. How do we know our children are doing what they are supposed to do in school? We show up, that's how. We show up at those orientations, open houses and parent teacher conferences. If we can make it to a couple of those PTA/PTO meetings, we show up there as well. Take advantage of every opportunity to be enlightened and made aware of what is taking place at the school and in the classroom. If we can send our children through those school doors five days a week for nine to ten months out of the year, can't we show up every now and then as well?

When we as parents show up, so do our children. We set the standard for the level of importance of education in our own homes. We display in action how education is valued. So not only do we show up at the schools, but we show up at the homework table as well. If we as parents don't show interest, care or concern in our children's education, why should they take heed to us advising them to do so? Actions speak louder than words. Free Ride to College is a call to action. It is a call to be proactive rather than reactive.

-It's better late than never

If you haven't been as involved in your child's education as you should have or would have liked to have been, it's not too late to start. No time for pity parties, excuses or to even beat yourself up. This is when the old cliché, "It's better late than never," actually has value. We do better when we know better.

As parents, we may find ourselves having to reset our priorities. Our children's education should be somewhere at the top of the list if not first. If we are showing up at the school and at the homework table, then we will be privy to the areas of study in which our children may be having issues with. With today's learning formulas and curriculum, we as parents may sometimes feel as if we need to visit our local community college to brush up on some things in order to even help our children with their homework. Another more realistic and economical option is that if your child is behind in math, science and/or writing and reading, get a tutor. It is cheaper than the former. Your child can do the work once they learn it; they just have to learn it!

I have used and recommend www.TechTutorsOnline.com. They are experts in their respective disciplines and have amazingly engaging tutors. They have rave reviews from almost every parent and student that have used their services. In addition, they are affordable and convenient.

Getting and Staying Ahead of the Game-Important Conclusions

In addition to being a parent, like I mentioned before, I am an educator as well; most of the time as a substitute teacher. Being a substitute gives me a comprehensive experience in all types of schools and their culture. I have had the opportunity to compare charter, private, Christian, low performing public and high performing public schools. This has given me a diverse perspective on educating students. This was also the foundation of my realizing that my responsibility as a parent was to provide an extension of learning at home from the things my children were doing in the classroom. The school is our partner in educating our children. Parents and teachers have to supplement one another. This is why it's important for parents to know what is taking place in the school and in the classroom. How else will we be able to reinforce it at home?

I am constantly reading about how to stay ahead of the game. Understanding the new skills that are needed to succeed in today's economy is critical. I recommend reading the following books: The World is Flat by Thomas Friedman and The Global Achievement Gap by Tony Wagner.

The World is Flat is a historical look at the United States shifting from an industrial base economy to a technology based economy. Reading The World is Flat and sharing the facts with my family vindicated me as the crazy parent that just wanted to torture her children by making them become math whizzes. It made me reevaluate where to steer my children academically.

Similarly, after reading The Global Achievement Gap, I engrained the following concepts from this book in my children so that they would become more competitive students:

- Critical thinking and problem-solving
- Collaboration across networks and leading by influence

- Initiative and entrepreneurialism
- Effective oral and written communication
- Accessing and analyzing information
- Curiosity and imagination

Allow me to add another important author whose books are a must read for parents. Malcolm Gladwell's most pertinent books for parents and students, in my opinion, are The Outliers: The Story of Success and The Tipping Point: How Little Things Can Make a Big Difference. In The Outliners, Gladwell makes a strong case for why children need to be able to communicate effectively with their superiors. He shows this with an intuitive story of why Korean Airlines had so many crashes in the 1990's. Now referred to as the "Cockpit Culture," it all boiled down to ineffective communicating between the subordinates, the co-pilots, and their superiors, the pilots, as a result of their culture.

Also in The Outliners, Gladwell explains another very important point about how doing something for 10,000 hours makes one an expert in any discipline. He tells the story of how Bill Gates' early exposure to computers propelled Gates into a unique advantage.

Last, but certainly not least, Proving Ground by David Tarver is a very good example of the 10,000 hour theory Gladwell explains. Proving Ground chronicles the journey to success of a lesser known outlier, David Tarver, who is just as shrewd as Bill Gates. From an early age, Tarver is exposed to and pursues a profound understanding of the evolution of digital technology.

Tarver's success is a result of the synergy of his father's expertise, tinkering with electronic equipment, competing in science fairs, unimpeachable work ethics and stellar academic accomplishments.

Tarver is exposed to equipment and skills that are a carryover from his father's experience as a communications expert in WWII. Although his father, like most Black men during those times, does not get the opportunity to cultivate his skills beyond the military. Instead, he nurtures a technological environment in his basement. Consequently, Tarver becomes the personification of an example of Malcolm Gladwell's The Outliers.

This 10,000 hours concept helped my kids to attain the full ride scholarships in two ways. I mentioned that my children are all engineers and engineering students, which means that they are good in math. I can assure you, they were not born with the ability to do math, but I was determined to get them as close to 10,000 hours of practicing math as possible. Just so you know, I did not announce to them, "Kids, we are going to practice math for 10,000 hours." Instead, I surreptitiously incorporated 10,000 hours of practicing math into their schedules. I sent them to tutoring once a week, I put them in math competitions, and I insisted that they were in the honors and Advance Placement math classes at school. This ultimately gave them competitive math aptitudes going into college.

My goal was to have them able to do complicated math problems in seconds without a calculator. So they practiced those skills over and over. The result was higher ACT math scores because they did not have to fumble around with calculators. The ACT is a time and accuracy test. Calculators slow students down. The higher your ACT score, the more scholarships you qualify for.

The 10,000 hour rule sounds like a lot, but you don't do it all at once. The key is to start early, like in elementary and middle school, and break it up into unnoticeable bits and keep building. So the saying that goes, "Practice makes perfect," applies here. It doesn't matter what your child's passion is-music, writing, math or science-they will become experts if they practice 10,000 hours.

Not Quite the End of the Road- How to Get Scholarships While in College

Although there are more scholarships available for graduating high school seniors, there are still lots of financial opportunities for college students. College students can take advantage of scholarships, paid internship and co-ops. Colleges have career fairs and companies come looking for the students that have a 3.0 GPA or better to hire in the summer. My kids have gotten internships that paid up to three thousand dollars per month, so keep your grades up.

The best place for college students to pursue scholarships is the departmental scholarships. The dean of your perspective college has great information and access to grants and scholarships for students in the department. So make sure that the dean of your college knows who you are and knows you need money. Moreover, just as high school seniors should have the scholarship documents ready at all times, so should college students, so they, too, can take advantage of scholarships and be prepared in advance.

A possible disadvantage for college students can be that they are very busy being studious making sure to keep their GPA up to maintain the scholarships they already have. It is imperative that college students manage their time wisely by making sure they use the breaks to update their profile information. College students should also ask for letters of recommendation from faculty as early as possible.

-More than one way to get there

This volume and forthcoming volumes chronicles ten years of my experience building competitive student profiles, which, I can't say enough, is the key to gaining admittance to the college of your choice and securing the money to finance your college expenses. As a tool to compliment these volumes I urge you to visit www.FreeRideToCollege.com/blog so that you can get frequent updates, get your questions answered and provide feedback. The information found on the website will not duplicate the information in the e-volumes, but instead serve as an additional tool and resource of information. I guess it's safe to say you can consider it a second means of transportation. So I suggest utilizing both, as they go hand in hand.

Www.FreeRideToCollege.com makes it easy to click through to resources via hyperlinks. The e-volumes and website are not just for parents and guardians. The information, resources, tools and techniques will help students get into the college of their choice and build a profile that will make them a competitive candidate for academic scholarships to colleges across the map.

Free Ride to College: A Guide to Grooming Your Kids For a Full Academic Scholarship is a comprehensive parent and student resource with recommendations for achieving a full scholarship to college. The main thing we as parents must understand is that our children's student profile will depend on how well we have prepared them as students. Again, although I make no guarantees, both the e-volumes and website will certainly provide the information to assist in making your child a competitive candidate for many scholarships.

See you next stop!